Krishna's Wonderful Pastimes

Falguni

ISBN 978-93-5559-237-8
© Falguni 2022
Published in India 2022 by Pencil

Contributors:
Editor: Anamika

A brand of
One Point Six Technologies Pvt. Ltd.
123, Building J2, Shram Seva Premises,
Wadala Truck Terminal, Wadala (E)
Mumbai 400037, Maharashtra, INDIA
E connect@thepencilapp.com
W www.thepencilapp.com

CONTENTS

The sound from the sky

King Ugrasena of Mathura had two children namely Devaki and Kansa. One demoness named Putna was nursing Kansa since his mother died. When Kansa grew as a young man, he had many demon friends. He wanted his sister to marry his human friend Vasudeva.Devaki agreed. Kansa thought he could be the King now but he couldn't. King Ugrasena didn't want Kansa to become the king due to his ruthless behaviour. As a result, Kansa put his father in prison and became the King of Mathura.

After Devaki and Vasudeva's marriage, he told the chariot driver," I will drive the chariot for Devaki". He obeyed and Kansa went. While taking Devaki and Vasudeva home, he heard a sound from the sky.

It was Akashvani. She told him, "Devaki's 8th child will kill you" and disappeared. Hearing this, Kansa removed his sword to kill Devaki but Vasudeva stopped Kansa and promised to give every child to him.

Kansa did not believe them and prisoned them too. The first 6 children born to Devaki were killed by Kansa. The 7th child's birth date was very near. Rohini, Vasudeva's first wife, came to meet Devaki on that day. As soon as he was born, Rohini took him to Mother Yashoda's house for safety. He was named Balarama.

Birth of lord Krishna

Some months passed away and another child was born. It was midnight and all the soldiers were sleeping. Suddenly their chains and the doors of the prison opened. Akashvani told Vasudeva to give the child to his friend's wife Yashoda and take the girl born to her.

He obeyed her. To go to Nanda's (Yashoda's husband) house, he needed to cross the river Yamuna. The river was over flooded. There was no chance to cross it. But as the child was an incarnation of lord Vishnu, the river split into two and gave way. While coming back, it stopped flooding and Vasudeva safely returned to the prison with Yashoda's daughter.

The doors of the prison closed and the chains locked them again. The soldiers heard the small girl crying and informed Kansa about the birth of the 8th child.

When he was going to kill her, she slipped out of his hands and said, "The boy which is going to kill you is already born and is safe" and disappeared. The boy was named Krishna.

Killing of Putna

After some days, Putna, a witch who knew sinful methods to kill small children entered Krishna's village glamoured a beautiful lady with a flower in a hand and poison in her breast. She had killed all the children born within 10 days. When she entered Krishna's home, Yashoda and Rohini were attracted to her and let her in. By seeing Putna, Krishna got to know that she came there to kill him. When he drank Putna's milk he also sucked her life air out and she fell on the ground breaking the trees within 12 miles.

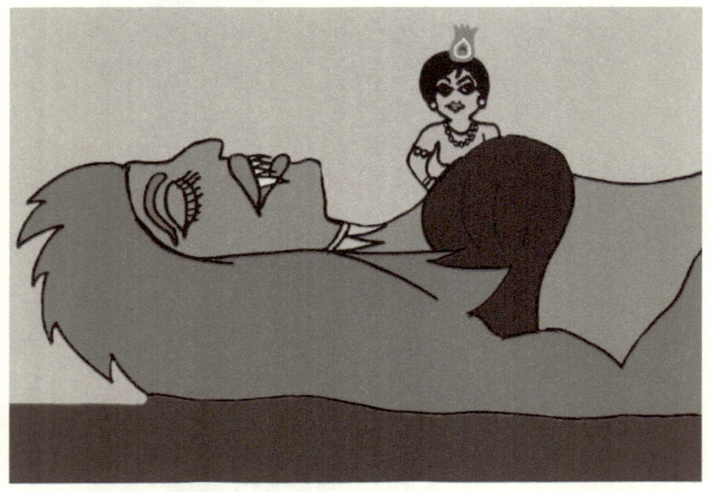

Salvation of Trinavarta

Few hours later, after Kansa got the message that Putna got killed, he sent Trinavarta the tornado demon to kill him. Trinavarta went to Gokul, saw Krishna, picked him up and then they fought against each other. While fighting Krishna got as heavy as a mountain. Trinavarta fell down and died.

The Universe

One day, Krishna ate some mud so Balarama complained Mother Yashoda.When Mother Yashoda told Krishna to open his mouth and he opened it, she saw the universe.

Demon cart

On Krishna's birthday, all the qualified Brahmans were invited. While they were chanting the hymns, Krishna fell asleep. Mother Yashoda put him in a cart nearby. That cart was actually a demon. Krishna struck his feet to the wheel of the cart and the cart collapsed with a great noise and the demon got killed.

Lucky fruit vendor

One day, a fruit vendor came to Maharaja Nanda's house. Krishna came outside running with grains in his hands. But some of them fell down and he got sad. But then the fruit vendor affectionately took the grains which were left in his hands and gave him as many fruits he wanted. Soon the fruits which were left in the basket turned into gold.

Killing of Vatsasura and Bakasura

1. Vatsasura

While Krishna and his friends were playing, Vatsasura, being a calf, came to kill Krishna. Krishna knew that he was Vatsasura. While playing he threw him in the air and he went far away and died.

2. Bakasura

Once a bird demon named Bakasura was sent by Kansa. As he reached Krishna he swallowed him. Krishna tried to tear his neck but then he spit him out. Krishna climbed to his beak and tore it apart.

Killing of Aghasura

Aghasura, a snake demon, came to Gokul. He opened his mouth and it looked like a cave. Krishna's friends went to discover the 'cave'. When Krishna saw him he tried to stop his friends but they were too far. He himself went into Aghasura's mouth and saw that his friends are going to fall in the snake's poison. So he tore Aghasura's skin and his friends were free.

Killing of Pralambasura

Pralambasura, one of Kansa's demons went to Agnidyetya. After that he told the mission given by Kansa and they both moved to the forest where Krishna and his friend's cows were grazing grass. Agnidyetya put fire on the trees and Pralambasura glamoured as a small boy went to Krishna and his friends when they were playing. He somehow took to the forest where the cows were grazing. Balarama, Krishna's big brother got to know that Pralambasura was a demon and then he killed Pralambasura.

Krishna sent his friends to sleep and swallowed the fire, even Agnidyetya was swallowed.

Lord Brahma's test

After that Lord Brahma came to Earth and saw that Aghasura was killed. He got to know that Krishna did it but forgot that Krishna was the 8th avatar of lord Vishnu. He tried to test Krishna. By his swan dust he could make anybody sleep. He put some swan dust on his friends while Krishna was far away and took them to Brahma lok. When he came back he saw that they were not there. Some swan dust had fallen on plants so he understood that Brahma did this all.

Krishna then multiplied his body and they took form of his friends and all went to their houses. After 1 year Lord Brahma came to see what Krishna was doing without his friends and saw that they were all playing. He was astonished at how they are all on Earth! He had been certain he had them in Brahmalok sleeping peacefully. Then he realized that Krishna was Lord Vishnu and gave his friends back.

Govardhana Hill Worshiped

Once in a year, people of Gokul had Lord Indra's puja. That day, Krishna asked his father, "Why do we do Lord Indra's puja, father?"Nanda replied, "Lord Indra gives us rain and rain is necessary for the plants to grow."Then Krishna announced that if we want to worship why not woship Govardhana Hill, which gives us land th grow crops, and cows, who give us milk.He convinced the people to worship them instead of Lord Indra. Hearing this, Lord Indra got angry and made a storm. To save everyone, Krishna broke the ground and picked up the hill on his little finger.

Everyone helped him by supporting the hill with their staffs. He also played his flute during the time. After 7 days the storm stopped and everyone was safe.

Kaliya nag, the five headed snake

Krishna and his friends were playing near the Ganga River. Suddenly, the water was becoming black. Everybody, even the plants were falling. Krishna took his friends to safety and saw a snake and he fought with him. Everybody gathered and saw him fight. Krishna calmed the snake and all the poison was gone and then he could clearly see. The snake's name was Kaliya. Krishna told him to go to the ocean but he insisted that the eagle would harm him. Krishna assured him," He won't harm you till he sees my footprints on your head."

About the Author

Name: Falguni

Book no.:1

I wrote this book at the age of 12-13. After reading many books of Lord Krishna I wrote this book. The next book I am going to publish is 'The 5 fairy tales' . I hope you liked this book. Some fun activities are given on the next chapter.(Just to see how well you red the book)

Activities for Children

<u>Questions and Answers</u>

Q : How many children did King Ugrasena had?

A : _______________________________

Q : What were their names?

A :_______________________________

Q : Who was Vasudeva?

A :_______________________________

Q : How many children did Devaki and Vasudeva had?

A :_______________________________

Q : Name the last child born to them.

A :_______________________________

Q : Who was Vasudeva's first wife?

A :_______________________________

Q : Who was Balarama?

A :___________________________________

Q : Who was the first demon/demoness came to kill Krishna in Gokul?

A :___________________________________

<u>Match the Following</u>

1) Krishna   a. Yashoda

2) Vasudeva   b. Balarama

3) Nanda   c. Devaki